TENDER REVOLUTIONS

John D. Thompson

First Edition

PALINDROME PUBLISHING
Des Moines, Iowa

———○———

Manufactured in the United States of America
Library of Congress Catalogue Number: 2002107385
ISBN: 0-9720717-0-9
Cover and layout design: Karisa Runkel

Palindrome Publishing
Des Moines, IA
515-274-3888/fax 515-265-3044
E-mail author at: jay_thompsonpoet@yahoo.com
Author can be reached by the above phone number or e-mail
for book sales, signings, and readings.

Manufactured by Sheridan Books, Inc.

THIS BOOK IS DEDICATED TO

DEAN DAWSON, A SELFLESS MAN;

BUBBA MCCOY, A GOOD BOY;

AND C. PAUL THOMPSON, MY FATHER.

Angel Tree,
Sprout, spread, then shed
Winged leaves
Full-circle, the evolution

Children of the woodland green,
Year-to-year
Earn your rings
Savor the tender revolutions

NOTES

Triskaidekic verse from the poem *Heart as Sponge*
is my own invention. It consists of 13 lines & 13 syllables
per line. The third line must have the number "1"
and the tenth line must have the number "3".
The rhyme pattern is AA, BB with corresponding
interior rhyme. The last line must rhyme with the tenth.
The title must have thirteen characters.
Triskaidekaphobia is fear of the number "13".

**The *gross poem* is another invention introduced
in this book and appears in the poem *Take One Dozen*.
This form poetry consists of 12 lines & 12 syllables per line
written as couplets. The title must be 12 characters; rhyme scheme
is uniform AA. Modifiers of the number *12*, such as *dozen*
and *twelfth* must appear twice in the verse.
Note the special page placement of the poem
in the book in relation to one definition of the word *gross*.

TABLE OF CONTENTS

FIRST-DEGREE TURNS

TABLE OF CONTENTS

SECOND-DEGREE TURNS

TABLE OF CONTENTS

THIRD-DEGREE TURNS

FIRST-DEGREE TURNS

LAST NIGHT AT THE BOW & ARROW PUB

My first night in the beer hall
Last night, last call for the tavern…

A weary archer missing most of the day's targets,
I pull my limbs into the Bow & Arrow Pub,
A Cambridge classic hugging the curbside
Turn Of Massachusetts Avenue,
Neo-gothic storefront in struggling neon,
Castle on the square,
Makeshift arena for fist fights and pseudo-intellectual debates.

The fluorescent bulb in the oaken cove
Dims with each passing candidate for cirrhosis
Entering, egressing.
Outside, yellow hydraulics
Of construction and destruction sleep upright
Like workhorses waiting for sunup's eight-hour ride,
Their mounts bracing the Bow for final execution.

I lay my quiver on a fraying leather stool,
Tripods marked by the buttocks of Boston,
The transient derrieres of Harvard Square,
Cock feathers and hen feathers,
Light conversations for a lethargic evening.
Pinballs bounce sprite, spontaneous melodies,
Hendrix jimmying on the jukebox,
The dying joining the dead.

A factory of kegs works the south wall,
Spigots pulling down the final shift,
An olfactory assembly line,
Vintage cigars and brandy
Toasting to the quail of Auld Lang Syne.

I order an ale for my ailments;
Faded banners hang from a bar-length mirror.
The crimson metastasizes to a dull purple with yellowing decals--
Too much smoke, too much football.

I remove my gauntlets and inquire of the bar keep
Where Matt Damon sat during filming.
Then I unravel his puzzled brow,
Will Hunting, I retort, *Good Will Hunting.*
His angular index points to the darkest escape of the room.

The director wanted total control of the light, he explains,
Proudly crediting himself for a brief bout with cinematography.

A portrait of John Jr. nowhere and everywhere on the walls,
A comic strip with Snoopy supine on his doghouse--waiting for a Woodstock concert ,
The Occurrence in three's.
He wanted total control of the light, I tell my Samuel Adams.
Who doesn't?

HURTING OUR PARENTS

Contusions of the womb,
wee breach our first contract
at the inchoate contact of birth.
The collective Child Harold,
our minds undress the repressed
Oedipal and Electra Complexes
to sleep slain forever
with Father Thyme
as wee smother Mother Earth
with enuretic pillows.

La Primera Mentira,
s-h-h (the first lie)
usually involves a stray puppy,
the neighbor boy,
or jewelry intended for posterity
sold for the pettiest of cash.

On Christmas eve,
wee disclose our knowledge
of the presents in the closet
& Santa's brandy of preference
among the pantry stash.

Whether it's Bombeck on the airwaves,
Loretta crooning about coal mines,
or Mom crying in a crusted apron,
wee learn that children can break a woman's heart
more decisively than the comeliest of men.

Wee commit the seven deadly sins
before the age of seven,
then enter puberty
& shatter the prohibitions again.

HEART AS SPONGE

the heart is a sponge obsessed with its own absorption

when its vessel is young, the guide is blind misfortune

"1" slip of the tongue, and the organ receives a squeeze

you wring what's left to be hung like wet sleeves in the breeze

at tension--at ease...the beating exceeds proportion

white serum taps to appease gods craving their portions

on and off the valves turn through permeated channels

Porifera's lovers learn to sink or swim canals

drained of their fill, the still-standing reduced to crawling

time's a pleasure to kill; "3" wishes before falling:

to live, to laugh, and to dream wherever desire flows

people soaking in schemes is the greatest story told

love is but a spill, so what is the use in bawling

*triskaidekic verse

KITCHEN SINK

I wake
& dress
in raiments
of *Winter Trees*.

At last,
Morning Song
lip-synchs
a dirge ironic.

The oven door,
Daddy's visage.
It will do.
It will do.

The pipe,
his tongue.
The gas gives him
b r e a t h.

I inhale.
He slips on
my head,
this old black shoe.

DRAWINGS

for Josh & Marian

I am drawn to white,
itinerant occupant of the sky,
color of the shell
circumnavigating the
seascapes of my eyes,
the   absence
of what is written,
the background
foreshadowing the story
on the page.
I suckle the cream
from the bosom which
will Oil-of-Olay age.
The final passage
of heated coal,
urban noise, DeLillo's word,
the undetected plague
entering the lungs,
Munch's *The Scream*,
the chiaroscurist's version,
on the bridge, a nervous bird.
The calcined hands
of the man at the
construction site.
The recitation of
the dream-destined,
Star Light, Star Bright.
The alabaster dimples
beneath the temples
of Shirley Temple,
the pachyderm's
ivory nose.
The names of the
unborn daughters
in the reluctant seed's garden,
Pale Hyacinth,
Skittish Lily, &
Albino Rose.

It is past my Homecoming.
Papers of tissue
fly like strings of doves
on the turning trees
outside the Learning Gate.
Time divides the prime of season,
separation of church and state.
I am drawn to the ghostmarm's chamber
beyond the fight songs
and psalms of hate
scribbled on the one-sided walk.
I've been drawn
by the winged sheets of memory.
Drink me, Liberty. Feed me chalk.

STREET SOIREE

for Bruce

Between Tremont and tomorrow
the ground smells like it should
just before the nascence of rain—
pluvial perhaps.
The city moves its concrete
glacier meticulously
during the high-speed
lull of traffic.

The burning oils downstream
this port of the Charles
light poems
beneath undulating candles.
Reminds me--
Widener opens at nine
one door at a time.

In fourteen minutes
we will disperse,
an adjourned jury
of jaded grammarians
& a Guggenheim foreman.

In a fortnight
from Logan,
cohort-aircraft will bank
an unforgettable deposit
into the World Trade Center
& not a scholar in Cambridge
to stop it.

A near hush falls
like a grievous angel
over our loquacious soiree.
The penultimate subject is the bomb;
I suggest we drop it.

THE POISE OF OCTOBER

for Jan

The game is at home.
I awake to the satin blues
of Sunday ritual.
The boxed-seat
balcony corsaged
in the chrysanthemums
of an autumn in extra innings.
Equanimity stretches
during the seventh chime.

I enter the open air
of random, iconic
terror delayed
due to the clemency
of soft weather.
The sermons & pep talks
on cappuccino break
nine stories & several newsbreaks
below my pointless view.

The hour of susepension
remiss without light-calorie jazz
spreading its sweetness
from the amplified unseen.
The shell-world in a series
of foul balls breaking windows
with no shatter of glass.
From here, I foresee
& prognosticate the next pitch,
but I am never asked.

The fray had gone seven.
The echoes of pinstriped ghosts
ticker-tape from the terrace,
a holier-than-thou Carey's cow
heroes' parade.
I recline like a Goya nude, war-bonded,
atop a take-me-out-
to-the-ballgame baby grand—
The best of season, best of show
MVPatriot trophy in hand.

ROUTINE

for Bubba

The bell tower broken
Its face unmoved
By the execution of dawn
The campus hills await
Morning reveille
From a bugle-snout
That blows no more
A villa of books
& beer cans remain asleep
Two feet stand over
The murmur of a fallen four

Master, just once
Let me be the master
I command you
To lift me from this place
Feed me a Big Scary Kitty Cookie
From the Three Dog Bakery for the unsniffed trail
Then cover my favorite blanket
Over your favorite face

For your every day
I must live seven
A dog is born to race with age
I've a nose nuzzling toward the fenceless yard
Free from the monotony of Purina
& the boundary of the kennel-cage

Master, this once
Let me play the master
Go and fetch my beloved toy
When you return, I will be gone
But you will hear howling
In the silence
Of my disappearance

Good boy…good boy

THE EVOLUTION OF MIRACLES

One pill
& you're a rock star.
Read the label, Alice.
The print is small.
Fame is elusive
like a rabbit.
Go on & grab it.
Have a cotton ball.
Surrealstic pillows smother
the valley of the one-hit wonder dolls.

A coven of groupies looking for Grace
after the hardcore encore,
witches of the hunt warm their cold ones
for somebody to love.
The split-match extinguished,
every hare in place,
The Airplane lands a contract.
It's a rebel bird in the plain
of a Manilow miracle.
The red-eye octopus riding
to a sensation overnight,
Jefferson Starship maneuvers from above.
Slick's orgasmic backing vocals
of the closest encounter edited for radio.
EDIT: The extended version wasn't long enough.

The ME decennium is for the last standing soloist.
Exit the dragon, enter Balin's ballads.
The ruby tentacles now wear prescription shoes.
Betty Ford is not the only celeb in rehab.
Even first ladies of rock-n-roll get the blues.
Starship sheds syllabic weight for Sara.
Nothing stops a cultured storm from the 60s
knee deep in its own attitude.

FROM *THE BOOK OF ANSWERS*

The Graces are ablaze & the moon is blue.
Fecundity's dust rises to abort the sky,
a eulogy for the philosophers' stone
inhumed in the plot of my eye.
Elmo's spire is electric,
raising its guard to the nemesis of dawn.
Blue feathers tickle across the airwaves' lawn.
I stroke cum genius from the River of Styx
& come-sail-away on a horse
dog-paddling in freshly poured Old Paint.
Now, who is this anchor's patron saint?

FECKLESS

Downsized in a Mom-sans-Pop store,
I am the Seen stealing a box of organized
valentines notorious for massacring Christmas
with crimps of redolent tissue, the color of bro-
ken hearts, their corpses outlined
in cracks of discounted gold.

I remand the Shutters of Surveillance,
Picture me under arrest!
Burn me over the hearth of retail injustice!

The Personification of Osteoporosis
scoops peanut clusters in silence
behind the window to a diabetic's cheating soul.
The shop is inert with gaseous nonchalance.
I am free to go but taxed for my wants.

The door knocks on me as I drizzle out.
Looks like pain, feels like doubt.

BEAUTY & THE BINGO

for Vickie

I am through keeping secrets, the clandestine canine restless,
the surreptitious beast prepared for the women's winter feast.

Five down & soon to B6,
I stood outside the hair house
& waited for mother's bouiffant
to rise for the occasion.

It was the Sixties
& women in their thirties
with metal helmets
& tongues of aerosol
sprayed & spoke of stratagem
in a hush-a-bye war,
a few no-good-men, the weekly casualties.

Jackie was a paper widow,
Twiggy, in vogue,
& a pixie I knew as Petunia
sang of the joys of being *Downtown*.
Five diagonal lights beamed
S
    A
       L
          O
             N   across my brow.

A caked doughnut from Rita's Coffee Shoppe,
igneous rock in my hand,
the hood of my corduroy jacket
dangling like an anachronism
in the final whiskers of October,
I balanced my salivant desire on hind legs
to enter the blue-warm atmosphere
of simmering gossip,
a doggie in the window
making snow angels in the wind
to hold back the forces of winter and going home.

Sarah, the head stylist,
with dorsal eyes and wisdom
stretching across county lines,
gave me a wink in the mirror,
an invitation to free space.

Upon entry, my owner
grabbed me by the nape-collar
as if to say, *Not ever & not now.*
Come along, Bingo Boy,
The Voice tempered behind its glass,
game over, tail home, or no puppy chow.

ENDS IN O

I found your common celebrity on an unpaved street in Baltimore.
Catatonic to your suffering, yet this corpse I could not ignore.
The wane of your wax-eyes bemoaned *The Bells*; silver between your teeth told of *Eldorado*.
I am not Annabel Lee; you're no Edgar Allan Poe.

The literate crave their heroes; poets beget their prizes.
A specious sun-god fed you golden apples filled with the souls of futile sacrifices.
I tried to warn you of this mythical haven, but I lost the moons to keep you in my shadow.
Alas, I am not Venus; you're no Apollo.

I sailed to Spain just to turn the century, circumnavigating for a truism.
My vessel overwhelmed by post-impressions, the stern punctured by the angled waves of cubism.
The Blue Period begins at sea; the dyad of our dimensions met but failed to get to the crucial tertiary flow.
I am not an obscure masterpiece; you're no Picasso.

I was searching for the music or perhaps looking for the money.
I wrapped best intentions around your ischium of gold clinging to me like virgin honey.
I was to be your Memphis belle; southern-fried dreams are wishbones too ironbound to swallow.
I am not Priscilla, the Queen of Graceland; you no gyration-sensation from Tupelo.

Last night you inebriated our home with envy; murder seduced your mind.
I woke grasped in the fists of suspicion; the wind of my pipe destined to unwind.
I fought back like Hippolyta of the Amazons; your determined green breathed its last to yellow.
I will not die as Desdemona; you'll not live as Othello.

You studied to paint my face; dapple-dab, your invention made me frown.
My sole request, lips of vineyard red; you plaster-pelted me in earth-stone brown.
I refused to fissure a smile, a woman of the lonesome frame, not one for sitting solo.
I am not Mona Lisa; you're no Leonardo.

You bade to decorate the place, frescoes of nude angels, the aerial attack.
We agreed Rome needed higher Renaissance in its art.
To achieve beyond the means at open hand; we assumed the requisite positions, both working on our backs.

From *The Creation* to *The Last Judgment*, our Florentine graffiti walled us in immortality.
The rooms were only ours to borrow.
I am not the Sistine Chapel; you're no Michelangelo.

OFFERING PLATE

The sanctuary, a repository
storing souls
one hour a week.
Agape, rejoicing,
we bring in the sheaves
with our cluster of tongues.

The hymnals sprout
paper wings.
Shame anoints minds
mired in secular things.

A child pilfers a dollar
from St. Peter's pan of gold.
The angel-eye of his father
catches the act of abomination.
He leans and tells
the shoulder of the abducted,

Do not transgress on the Lord's time.

The infernal voice of
his testimonial brother,
sibilant Old Serpent,
advises the other side
of the boy's shrugger,

If you're going to ssssssin, make it a five.

OH

Obelisks of obsidian
Occluding oyster-like opalescence
Onerous omens
Officiously obviating others
Ominously opaque
Oneiric overtures

SPINNERS

5
Spin doctors
A remedy of rhythm
Sure cure for the blues
Motown pops who are tops
Could It Be I'm Falling
In Love With
You
?

ENDYMION'S DREAM

somnum ei inductum

I awake & cry out for Selene
in a moonless sky
spelling out in stars,
My love, goodbye.
In a world without mirrors
I rely on the trespass of waters
for knowledge & truth,
of the endurance of youth,
& the whereabouts
of my fifty daughters.
I crawl from the cave
of somnolence deep
to gather wool
from barking sheep.
My canine inverts.
At the earth's core he bays.
I move to look for the lost Harps,
but he commands that I stay.
Open, Thessaly, from where I fled.
The Muses are living, but their song is dead.
I've the keys to their city
but cannot find the gate. Only
achromatic illusions open & close
in this hypnagogic state.

Morpheus' spell is Hypnos' to keep.
In here, the god of dreams is the god of sleep.

BONE AND SALT

I hesitated and thought
to lag back for you;
but such ceremony
would cause this frame
of bone to turn
into a floorboard of salt.
If you were to blame,
it would be my fault.

I paused to contemplate
the consequence of the gesture,
my neck pirouetted
for these eyes to analyze
your behind-the-back conjecture.

Connective tissue
to bitter grains.
First it pours,
then it rains.

The Name of the Star

for Kent & Clay

I have confused
This house of purloined shoes
For a city of dreams,
The robust of red
For emerald's ebullience
& the road of caution in between

I've mistaken archetypes
—the nature of things—
For paradigms
—the order of things—
In the procession of strangers
Offering mantras
Like home, like home

Like Gloria & Gaynor,
I have survived
The sleeping rust of tin,
A stroke of heartless men
I've swallowed their pride
& spat into the sunset's den

I am timorous of wheat
What lies among the chaff
My uncle's petting zoo
The hired hands of his staff

I've misnamed
Dorothy's lament
For Dorothy Lamour,
Judy's for Ruby's,
Piece-fluff for film noir
& falsely attributed
Hollywood glamour
To any Gabor

I have lost my flat star
& found a garland
Of Cabbage Patch babies,
Song-and-dance men
Confident as maybe's

Where are the Randy Newman protesters,
the Munchkins who warble and act?

It is I & a gay dog
In the euphoria of kaleidoscope-fog
& a brief bevy of witches
who passed acting class

WHISTLER'S LIPS

You indigenously own one
To fetch the canine home
You purchase to purse more of them
Silver slips of the tongue
To regulate the warring fields
To sound the four-course hour
To cry, *Vortex in the clouds*
Across an eight-man Nebraska town

If the long-legged condition
On the street is concupiscent,
This is the howl
From an elevated steel bar
The call of the wild construction worker
Arrangement in grey and black
Portrait of a Porcine Chauvinist

Like its downstairs dweller
    The hum
A whistle is the neutral zone
Between the verbal and not so
Quasi-speaking, pseudo-showing
Desire's intent to be discontent
Just make a wish and   *b*

    l

    o

    w

ICTUS AND BREVE

Ictus and Breve
A point well taken
Cushion the blow
Of an oncoming word
Acccent, soften
What is stirred or shaken
Distress on the stresses
Until the music is heard

Ictus and Breve
The parents of meter
Siblings to syllables
Relatives to rhyme
Spicing the vocables
To make the phrase sweeter
A puncture and pillow
To the lay of the line

ackity-ack-ack

only if
you leave me
will I ever
get you back

nourish, sustain
       sustain, attack

it takes a child
to raze a village
it takes an eye
to spy the stacked

nourish, sustain
       sustain, attack

the camel breaks
from press of water
the arid straw
mends his back

nourish, sustain
       sustain, attack

this game of chess
quotidian Technicolor
black takes white
white takes black

nourish, sustain
       sustain, attack

how   far
from this house of local color
until your pail becomes a bucket,
my brown bag pales into a sack

nourish, sustain
       sustain, attack

2

SECOND-DEGREE TURNS

SHELL GAMES

I entered your Psyche
With & without
Permission, contrition
The open, Fallopian
Appended by the liquid tubes
Of impregnable dreams.

Like my childhood,
I had this summer
All to myself;
But I confused solstice
With equinox
& cleaned you for spring.

I found Methuselah's movies
Reeling behind your left ear.
You retrieved the sound's dialogue
On dates with forbidden concessions
When the moment struck you
Numb & dumb.

Fissures here, schisms there
Delineating the coastal shores
Of jealousy waiting to harbor;
But it was she
Who took you to school
In her hothouse waters.

Inside your head
I became invisible, indecipherable
As I studied how you studied
Scarcely room for one of us
To pass the exam.

So many shells
Under one nut
Absorb in the brain,
Think with your gut.

You found your sex
& proclaimed it complex.
Limn the limb, feel like a swim?
Wait an hour after eating
Then dive in.
Banging bones, does it hurt
When she waists her drop-cloth skirt?

If I stepped out through your eye,
Could you compare us?
I remain in your core.
You're not hurt; you are Sore —
& I, limbic one,
Am   Eros.

INSOUCIANCE & BENCH REST

I.

Luxury is lying on my lap
telling easeful untruths,
keeping me wretchedly comfortable,
ensconced in these pillows and shams.
These goosefeathers are horsefeathers!
I canter beneath ruptured wings
& V-fly above luckless shoes.

II.

Dough rises judiciously
in the kitchen court.
Witness, butcher and baker.
Crocker takes Hines
behind the salt shaker.
From the two-fisted gavel
of, *Yes, do it again!*
Gluttony is temperate.
Carnal cooking is sin.
Yeast falls on its knees.
The leavened levitate,
again born again.

Dough rises judiciously
from the folded robes
of fluted sleeves.
The Loaves of God
mold by the dozen
in the refrigerated section
of the Tower's deepest frieze.

$

Money is clear to me.
I precipitate through its lucidity,
diaphanous in its deeds,
sheer power the effect.

I am carded by its gossamer authority,
indebted to its credit,
sold on the Invisible Sell.

Permanent residence
for posthumous presidents,
Money is bald,
heir-overdue,
securities in overt extensions,
BMW bangs,
cash-cow curls,
roots of affluency
with parting interest.

Money is on the air,
FM in the AM.
The wealthy wake up late
& furphone in
to coin a phrase.
Money is wavelength
& we can see forever
on a clear day.

TAKE ONE DOZEN

The gesture of obsession, furtive as spy,
sneaks up in front of me without meeting my eye.

The absence of possession, pastry in the sky,
I will take one dozen but don't ask me to buy.

The witless at confession, papal alibi,
Words in the wrong ear effect   knees to cry.
                     skinned, sinned

The laxity of tension, zealous easy ride,
Break from the crate, goslings, or prepare for the Fry.

Arthritic joints in session, Congress won't prescribe;
warfare for welfare or give the carpals a try.

The twelfth-day of winter, my true love said goodbye.
Fey gestures of obsession greet another eye.

** gross poem

On the Subway with Bernhard Goetz

If I look through the dark shaft
as if the desire to perform fellatio
has overcome my fear, perhaps
his instrument will raise acutely
& miss killing the music
of this cruel quartet.

The subway is a stream
of unconscious characters,
unflinching fish, unfeeling waves.
His temper, trigger-happy;
the .38 starts spraying bullets
& spreading the news.

The late editions,
greased with a Smith & Wesson,
fold with the *Times*
to the floor with a clap.
Christmas three stops away,
the apple is goose-fat with vigilance
& vengeance.

...I'm leaving today.

MADNESS

Mad dogs remember where they took their last bite
Blood seeps into the spume of memory
To trigger the howls of lupine in white

Mad love remembers where it pursed its last kiss
Shaped in the labial onset of *perhaps*
The lips dislodge but never dismiss

Mad boys remember where they scarred the sad girls
On a closing school of clouds above the River of Screams
A silent shrill to straighten the most innocuous curl

Mad pols remember where the buried bodies live still
Leaving the All Saints decayed for a fresh Election Day
A victor-elect is born when the problem people are killed

Mad souls remember where the drenched ones were blessed
Extradited from the borders of sin
Examined with holy water and passing the test

A mad man remembers where he displaced child and wife
 Portraits of blame hung in charcoal and blue
The freeze-frame of regret snapping two times less than twice

Madness remembers where sanity took its last stand
In a fixed-fight arena ringing in the ears
A piebald arbitrator lifting mental illness by the ungloved hand

ONE SONS/TWO SON

A prodigal son
& a prodigious one
The former spending to save an insolvent dream
The latter spent on the debt of the first hand's cool steam

A given son
& a gifted one
The former inherits with nothing to prove
The latter is a mastermind merit, but it's never his move

An aggregate son
& an agreeable one
The former accumulating for its own sake
The latter replenishing the remains in his late wake

A dubious son
& a dutiful one
The former shadows himself and calls his lies shade
The latter gratefully labors in the gift of each day

A littoral son
& a literal one
The former sucking the ocean out of his family while standing ashore
The latter nailing tacks of brass on his enemies & marking the scores

A furthered son
& a farther one
The former given star pastures & excuses on set-aside reserve
The latter thrown out like a boomerang & told not return

A full-blown son
& a full-grown one
Each knows each as a brother
I am one, & I am another

WOMEN OF THE GLASS CEILING

Women of the glass ceiling
Gather at the Skywalk Lounge
To exchange morning gossip
Thumb to mouth,
Each lights a mummified tobacco
Ideas of promotion, self-expression
Convert to ashes
Before the waiter pours ice water
In their glasses & nerves

Women of the glass ceiling
Seem opaque to their supervisors
Who grind feminine minds
Then shred the evidence
& take the credit home
In a briefcase
To pay off the mortgage
Or garner whatever tokens of praise
He thinks her reclaimed efforts deserve

Women of the glass ceiling
Hide their bruises in hairdos
& keep the office injustices
For posterity in a mental file
To disclose in a tell-all biography
Of the abuse & corruption
Intelligence property abduction
Her story, a straight-&-narrow documentation
Of the 9-to-5 jolts and curves

Women of the glass ceiling
Conceal their frustrations
In replica-power suits
& spend the leftovers
Of their meal minutes
By speed walking in rubber souls,
Circling their collective loins of produce
Tableside the power lunch of man
Who cannot remember
When a better dish had been served

QUORUM

Allied and present,
we adjust our spine
one victim
one vertebra
at a time—
a cervical, whiplashed neck
my thoracic, broken heart
our lumbaric, jaded spirit
this sacral, busted ass.

Along the high backs
of oaken chairs,
PROPERTY OF THE STATE
we pop in the agenda
for the applicants
in absentia, their bark
pounded by the pause
of authority.

The hour's slight majority
seated by proxy,
crossing our legs
by invitation only,
morning stretch,
the inaugural exercise of power.
In unison, we breathe
in the frustration
of compensation contemplation.

How much for that stray tear
in the battered window
of a blackened eye?

One thousand, two thousand?
Can the sheltered blink, can she see?
Check the kitty of petty cash at the safe house
before we make it three .

HALFWAY HOME

Home Semi-Sweet Home

I step in; I step out
The arc-apex of middle space is halfway home
I am measured by the distance covered
Front leg first & heel to toe

I move in; I move out
The wheeling cargo is halfway home
I choose the path of most resistance
The miles gone are miles to go

I am in, & I am out
This passing fancy is halfway home
I am treaded by the vehicle of trend
Driven by those paving the road

I reach in; I reach out
Free hand in the kitchen jar, I'm halfway home
I take only what occupied time allows me
Clearing the shelf-gardens honest digs have grown

I walk in to first, then head out for third
Second base is halfway home
I want more than kisses from this diamond mound
A virgin-jewel thief on the prowl & probe

I breathe in; I breathe out
One last exhale; I'm halfway home
I have lived to be the death of me
Tripping over light, I fall on stone

ROLLING HEADS

Antoinettes of the agency,
we sustained on our
constituents' cake
& filled our burgeoning,
bourgeosie pensions
with petit four dreams
of retirement condominiums
in Haiti, Cayman,
the Tea Islands & the High Seas.

We centralized the intelligence.
It was the mode never
to disclose our mediocre mean.

Iscariots to the Twelfth Power,
or just asleep-at-the-throne's wheel?
The public's indignation was no way
to treat us powdering Queens.
The Palace of Versailles--
all aflutter like an Austrian hand fan--
batting its eyes at the sight of our heads
& the sounds of the guillotines.

COVET

Covet the players
Who post all the points
Covet the superstars
Who fill up the joints
Covet the long legs
Seducing your street
Covet accomplishment
Transcending mere feat
Covet the wife
Neighboring next door
Covet the hour
You make her a whore
Covet the souls
You think you have saved
Covet the sin
You twofer to your grave
Covet the trails
Other have paved
Covet because
All humans crave

SKIN

Wrap around bones
Burnt sierra and sandpaper
To the touchstone eye
Sun soaked and tested
By water, wind, and time
A cover longing
For exposure
The vision
Surpassed by the smell
Of the touch
Keep it lean
Replenish the bruised fruit
The produce
Always up for sale
Peel to find the leper
Clinging   to
The chafing layers inside
Its mouthpiece singing
Ian's *At Seventeen*
Fat folds like a lawn chair
On a waning beauty queen
Learn the truth
Janis tells
Should you strike oil
In those peek-a-boo-hoo wells

CHLAMYDIA

This is my daughter, Chlamydia
Akin to Gonorrhea
Street angel to Syphilis
I bear her every nine lovers or so
Bacterial swaddle in my uretha
A gift from one of three or four Magi
Painful pregnancy
Abortion via antibiotics
In my endless spin of promiscuity
She is born unborn again

The child keeps me under wraps
As I slide into the chill of the stirrups
My cervix offering itself to circumspect science
Spreading pamphlets on my barren plateau,
The doctor slaps my disease
One mommy
A diary of daddies
I leave her a test-tube orphan at the free clinic
This is my daughter, Chlamydia
Shake hands with the disposables, dear
Wear your pink gloves

2001: CHANDRA'S ODYSSEY

Gary needed space
Rooms not a ruse
To grow his vineyard
In the District

I kept my secret seed
In the Congressional closet
His charisma holding office
Close to my yearling heart

It is always hunting season
Among the reeds
Of L'Enfant's weeping meadow

Our affair was up for re-election
I was behind in the polls
So I spoke to him of strategy
The susurration of a child
To rock-a-bye the vote
Toward ignominious defeat

The missing are omniscient

Have you seen his July eyes?
The ice-water stare on page 87
Of *People Weekly* Vol. 56, No. 4?
Spooked by the future
As if he had witnessed
The second cumming
Of Lewinsky's dress

Psychics see me behind shrubs
My nude body in a furrow
Of soil, dark and tangled,
Like the surreptitious kisses locked
In my brown copse of curls

He was an animal attraction
& I a Modesto magnet
The Last Time I Saw Him
(The Motown metaphor ends here)
He pinned me against the icebox
Of his Adams Morgan brownstone of ambition
& whispered, *Cellar wine*

Our love story is hot
What I've shouldered remains cold
Temperature is irrelevant
In time, my pretty, in time

PENELOPE, NOT PERSEPHONE

It was Penelope, not Persephone
Who kept her head above Hell
But not piping water

Penelope who was the first to have a website
Weaving, unweaving, & waiting
For Odysseus to return

In his absence
Penelope was well suited
To shroud men seeking her favor

It was Penelope, not Persephone,
For whom no one hung portraits
Her face a caricature in the gallery of Troy

Penelope once betrothed now betrayed
By her lover's memory of Queen Helen I
First love, first choice, first mate on a thousand ships

In her presence
Penelope reduced to a Homeric bridesmaid in a parlor
A twenty-year widow-in-waiting with Persuasion by her side & on her lips

MNEMOSYNE

All orphaned brides,
dressed in silent bells, draped in social condolences,
I am the prompt for the forgotten words
to your wedding song.
I, the daughter of Earth and Sky,
the recall of the past,
immaculately personified.
Lose me & you will forget this pain,
yet never discover joy.

I am a goddess from the Old School,
pre-Olympic love child,
lead singer of the Titans.
I enthrall even the greatest of gods.
Zeus lured me to make beautiful muses together--
nine letters, nine nights, nine lives, a-non.
Even I confuse my daughters with the Sirens.

Without me
humankind procreates
unable to name
or care for its children.
Your altar ego is my alter ego.
I literally keep you from becoming
fucking beasts.
Should I ever fade,
Calliope, my eldest, awaits on my wing.

*
Memory
Never
Escapes
Me,
Occluded
Nosegay
In
Cerebral
*
devices,
algorithmic schemata,
digital, antithetical
to otherwise
heuristic suffices.

I am—
Who am I?
Oh, yes, Mnemosyne.

Mother of the poetic line,
maid of honor in your mind,
attendant of the details,
enabler of enjoyment,
to the greater ceremony,
the grander scheme.
Discard the veil, these reins,
inhale the rain lifting,
gather the lingering bouquet.

ORNITHOMANCY FOR THE BYRDS

The Word of God penned perhaps
The best folk song of the 60s
An offering from the Old Testament
A verse from Ecclesiastes
Uplifting, a flit to the spirit
An of-a-feather flight of the soul

A song for all seasons
Triad of harmony from five beakless birds
Earth-bound creations
Soaring voices
A time to be timeless
A time for His Word

War birds hovered around Roger
To mute the music of peace
War birds hovered around Gene
And still the band crooned
War birds hovered around Chris
Yet the message was heard
War birds hovered around Mike
From here to the rice fields of Asia
War birds hovered around David
The Lord's children sang every word

Sons and daughters of the Beat Generation,
Turn on the recording
Turn to the passage
Turn to the meaning of the soft-rock 45
Descending from the seventh position of heaven
To top the pop chart,
Ascending to keep the last temptation alive

The word of God
Uplifting and winged
Rock-n-roll scripture
Nature procures its own art

The word of God
Uplifting and winged
Rock-n-roll scripture
New-age ecclesiarchs

The word of God
Uplifting and winged
Rock-n-roll scripture
Nesting in the heart

PRECIPICE BALL

Luna dipped to Hades—
Oh, hell,
The moon went to Hell

Astral acrobat,
Deep-well dweller,
& I with my dreams of cheese
Soon followed

Half-baked pies
Fell from the sky
As I lay crying
In Faulkner & Dante's
Unfinished tag-team novel,
A work in regress
Disfiguring my speech
By mixing metaphors
& true motives
With Molotov tears

Hope swung low
Like a funeral chariot
Carrying the dead-flesh
Of my expectations
To anxious graves
Hell has no free men
Except those still willing
To work for a non-living
God needs no free men
Leave former slaves

THOSE IN VITREOUS ABODES

Marriage is no bird
Feather-the-less, I threw stones
To ground the fly-about drake
Give Wedding her wings

An onyx to slay Status
& yoke him to my bosom,
A garnet to bleed Money
From the Stiff's coffers to my bone-sere springs

No fowl but two thrown
Alas, Grimm's bounty lies slain at my boots & bidding
A mother-goosed by the in-laws
To nurse, scour, & so

I have eaten her chirps
Yet Raven remains hungry
Every crow deserves crumbs
Every crumb deserves crow

—○—

DOOR KNOBS

My neighbors are doors
I ignore all but the knockings
Paneled decorations of cornhusked configurations
Or wreaths of starched berries
Mere pretense
To the spartan interiors of wallpapered nerves

Dulled by personas
I prefer to polish the apartment #'s
106 curses his lack of advancement
108 makes love to her tapes of yester-*Days of Our Lives*
111 is a couple trying too hard to conceive
112 places his rookie bride on injured reserve

An unabashed shamus chewing a shoe,
I wait for their warm prints on the brass globes
To extend an invitation into their private worlds
Giving eyes to my ears,
Their voices sound much different in their domains
Than the superficial tones they suggest when passing in the hall

I should be lobe-locked
My cochlea chained & elevated
To swing before the transom
Mindful of anything but my own business,
I lower my cheek to the open-mouth keyhole

The floor collects their dirt and my wax
A custodian-in-residence who hears and knows all

KEYS

Copper inmates
On a chain
Unable to set the ring free
A lock on lending a hand
To unqualified hands
Doors open
The day proceeds

THIRD-DEGREE TURNS

IMMORTELLE

A desiccant season in the turgid well.
The rich hold their form,
Immortelle.

Lady Terror stills for her portrait; this oil will sell.
A beast comes to market,
Immortelle.

A break in the day's business, cracks in Piper & Shell.
Sister Pisa leans in mercy,
Immortelle.

Blue the blood's mood & the Registry of such clientele,
Unshaken but stirred,
Immortelle.

The secret of dead flowers' undying —
Only Enya-time will tell.
The rarefied divide & collect
At Abraham's or Hades' table,
Immortelle, immortelle.

THE BELL CURVE

At the academy, my daughter broods upon a bell.
Her mind responds, salivates
to the Pavlovian rings.
The tintinnabulations take their diurnal toll.
Her aspirations and aptitude slide
along invisible convexes.
A lean to the right, advanced placement;
a lean to the left, remedial disgrace.

Her playmates become cohorts
bedecked with spectacles, laptops, and a plan.
Our Campanulate sauces homebaked essays;
salt with assertion, cinnamon with support.
To bed with no dessert
if she inks and plumes a non sequitur
her stepmother and I fail to understand.

I hire her a tutor
to teeter her toward college,
away from minimum wage.
Perhaps Barron, Kaplan, or *PR*
will assist us to raise the verbal fields
we are unable to yield at home.

Or perchance all our Angelus needs
to shift to a more auspicious distribution,
a lesson learned in time
when a girl grows curves of her own.

THANATOPHOBIA

I ambience my home
with the fear of death,
Swiss clocks
with pendulum-knives
carving out time.
I lie dead again
like the Bundren family matriarch
across caravan sheets
& stare at myopic eyes
of multiple first-persons
in the ceiling,
sealing my fate
with Plaster of Paris
& other affordable
French white wines.

Recumbent in my repose,
I peruse my week's work
section-by-section,
scanning the prolix columns
of fatuous self-advice.
I ponder my last movement--
Perhaps I will pull myself up
by these unseasonal garlands,
phone the sandman & postman,
then hang up twice.

I had preferred the anxiety of maturity
to be my phobia of choice,
no Lincoln-dollar word entry
in the reference ever to be found.

So I choose to become proactive,
universal, an interior decorator,
& design my supine occupancy
aboveboard before I register
in the blue tome
two-yard sticks underground.

FIN-DE-SIECLE: THE OTHER SIDE OF CELEBRATION

In Memphis
No blue tongue of a suede shoe
Spoke of Elvis
The night every song died
Save *Auld Lang Syne*
Graceland greeted its holiday visitors
With horns, hats, and banners
Flying at half-mast

In Hollywood
No theatre opened
For the fans of Monroe or Gable
A night for Lombardo
Not Lombard
The Brown Derby
Dipping its lid
To the last falling star

In New York City
No night owls rooted for the Yankees
The specters of DiMaggio and Mantle
Trading stolen bases like playing cards
From a section reserved for the Hall of Famed
Ruth at the plate and on the mound
Pitching himself
A dropping silver ball

The formal casualty of a century
Seals the anaerobic fate of one-hundred years
Giving birth to the promise
Of merely one
A parentless man
The fiction of bantam girls are his daughters
He prays for the softhearted beating
Of the next four-hundred seasons
To each bookmarked boy
Who will never be his son

SATELLITE DISH

The universe is a Venn diagram.
Dissect the intersections.
The Geometry of Astronomy is God's master plan.

Our galaxy (why not possess it?) is full
of child stars. Some become satellites,
ambassadors to Ghana or Mars.
Others are knighted as planets.
Despite the astronomical distinctions,
all must serve the sun.

Most beads string along sisters.
All planets are brothers,
concentric siblings circling about
their solar single parent,
moon daughters, global sons.

The unknown kin of Plato,
the Galilean analysanda of Jupiter,
the secret shards of Venus
be- passing -tween
Big and little Dips.

Astral family,
alignment of harmony,
partial light,
fractal darkness,
total eclipse.

PENUMBRA

All days become slaves serving the Grey
The guard of darkness permits me
To observe the capture of light
Falling from its summit like a conquered empire

Even the sun must cool

Given its last Sabbath and drinking Venus' wine
But no bread to store for the morrow
The iris bends to adjust for the eclipse
Passive flowers in their voices of witness
Unflinchingly gazing into the blinding shade

Even the eyes are fooled

The moon is an after-hours luminary
Mounted on its own marquee
Earth is an understudy still learning her lines
On a stool of deference
Behind the spherical curtain
With its cast of supporting shadows

Even the planets are ruled

TRIPLE-ENTENDRE

I am a rook
moving parallel
to the borders
of the gameboard.
I slide along longitudes,
survey the latitudes
to protect my king
& Empress my queen.
A mobile strategist,
I take on all inferior opposition
& remove them
piece by piece.

I am a rook
spreading my
black marble wings,
these smooth, feathered things.
My plumage unfolds
to reveal my collection
of ornaments
from the Old World.

I am rook.
How I scheme & I steal!
First, I feign
to live by The Book;
then fly, do what I feel.
My soul is a cheat.
Play my game.
Join the flight.
I've new players
to master
& fowl bedding to beat.

CREDIT

It was I who gave air to *Ariel*
A napalm of ideas
Birthing verse-flames from my head

It was I who wrote *Morning Song* in my sleep,
Taking plaudits for Plath
Now that Sylvia's dead

& it was I who charged the glass doors
With my cannon of cards to commandeer
Her repertoire of work on extended credit

& it was I who imbibed the explosive cocktail dry
The stories of her private war dowsed
With my stirred olives & signature edit

END TRAILS

I cannot tell time
But I can speak of death
Knocking like clockwork
On my watchtower head

I recognize the Reaper
My future is grim
His smile of silver
Scythes below my chin

This quietus trail
Digests its full course
I fall on my mount
To ride the Pale Horse

THE SCHEMING

In honor of Theodore Roethke

I think to scheme and take my scheming slow.
Sleep cannot disturb this perpetual mind
casting the players for upcoming shows.

The meditation, a most loathsome ode.
Syrup from my cerebrum salts your eyes.
I think to scheme and take my scheming slow.

You cannot break from this pernicious hold,
demure my lure, despair your prize. My line
casting the players for upcoming shows.

Your career is at a standstill, a new high-low.
I offer my card; solicit me anytime.
I think to scheme and take my scheming slow.

I study your dreams and know what you know.
You take direction stage left and receive what's condign
as my right brain casts players for upcoming shows.

An offer downstage, you upstage me and go.
The exit is an impasse. Someone should fix that sign.
I think to scheme and take my scheming slow,
casting the players for the late show.

MODEST TRAIL

I need to believe
The golden tablets will be found
Under a lowing sky, beneath higher ground
I need to believe
The purity of my church whitewashing all nations
That nothing was lost
During Smith's first translation
I need to believe
Moroni, fleet angel, would not steal
The Proof for the Ages
For safe keeping upstairs
Where gates & saints-in-waiting conceal
I need to believe
Brigham & his legacy propagated the ovaries of the West
With the scripted seeds from Palmyra,
Christianity is good; Mormonism is best
The faces of his chosen men
Buried & suckling on Polygamy's breast
If I cannot believe
I will break away
Reorganize, rethink
Forge a trail down Garden Grove way
When the call letters *RLDS*
On the AM no longer suffice
& college date rapes, divorce among my people
Exceed the national average twice
I will rename the denomination
A modest moniker would be nice
Community of Humility? Hushed Hope?
What the hell—
Community of Christ

THE SMOLDER OF OLD STONE

Iowa City, IA; November 20, 2001

The university like a map
is not the territory you once
blazed with fiery legislation,
the brim of a dream,
& the fervid promises of honest work.

This evening, abandon is a capital crime.
The news—*The Burning of Old Capitol*—
a grassfire sweeping across
the Pentacrest & prairie grass.
From the flame of tenured tongues
across the lectern to erudite neophytes
contemplating the smoldering of old stone.

It is the season of rescue;
we are all armed with water.
As your beheaded dome plunders,
heritage loses a tip of its golden touch.
The symbolism of a state dissipates.
The assignment for tomorrow is symbology,
but who has time to study it much?

Nuclear Family War

My family is still alive, damn it
The militant positioned to survive another era
Male progeny marching about in Oshkosh B'gosh
Denim straps clinging to their fading childhoods
The building of soldiers
One Tinker Toy at a time

Tomorrow's women in grandmother's bathroom
Discovering the joys of Lilt
Lathering and rinsing the angels
Out of their cirrus-cloud hair
Tiny mouths talking about the boys overseas
On the other side of the bathtub

Father is an oxygen tank
Gas in, gassed out
An army of one too mulish to follow his own orders
The general is still breathing
This POW checked while on holiday
I wonder, *Who will cut the cord on his accord?*

Mother surveys the remains like a reconnaissance pilot
She swoons about her peremptory rounds
Spot landing to dress unhealable wounds
Her countenance shows regret but no surrender
All the dead have survived, she reports to herself in her sleep
Too bad, though, about the living

THE PROSAIC

I spend Labor Day weekend tucking away whites
in bureaus of cedar and the bottoms
of his-and-whomever's linen closets.
Scenes from Love! Valour! Compassion!
play in off-black-and-white on the flowered wall.
The pennant races sharpen as I peruse
the *Life/Style* section to see
who is pitching the new fall line-up.

Monday is jejune rain. I am trapped
inside a Carpenters' song and darting
self-criticism. In tribute to Karen,
I skip lunch and smile. I have *underlined*
and italicized properly all summer long
and still did not wear August well.
The sweaters in my armoire begin
rustling for the winter.

SUI GENERIS

Who runs in the mill
with a fist full of grist?
Who scurries through
the sounds of pounding corn?

I have run in the mill.
I'm still running until
I am run-of-the-mill
no more.

GRIEVING MEADOW

Grief is a field most verdant in autumn's final episode.

I watch *The Sopranos* for the singing lessons.
A beautiful crime is music to my membranes.
Family dysfunction, a tympanic dirge.

This fall my mother appears
in her own cable series
HBO/Housewives Bound Obligatorily.

The producers toy with the show's title.
Celibate in the Country
tops The Table's short list.

Dad quit smoking last November.
The first leaf to turn,
the last oak notwithstanding.

It has been nine months
since the headlights
escorted him to Rose Hill.

Six Feet Under in its premier season.
Some of the town folk like the plot.
I look for the birth of his death
from his widow's fresh womb.

A PATHY

I.

A
Careless clouds strewn along a lethargic sky
Catch my otherwise inattentive eye
I pay no heed to what lives or dies
I slip on the negligee of negligence just for size
P
My otherwise inattentive eye catches light
Only darkness emits
Slipping on negligence just for size
I throw my stones and my fits
A
Only darkness emits
From the bleak house where I dwell
I throw my stones and my fits
My ear falls deaf to the street stories the town crier tells
T
From this bleak house where I dwell
The dismissive shutters close to the world outside
My ear falls deaf to the stories the crier tells
I speak in seclusion and there is where the truth lies
H
The shutters dismiss and close to the world outside
I pay no heed to what lives or dies
Talk of seclusion is where the truth lies
Beneath careless clouds strewn along a lethargic sky
Y

II.

Indifference is a sneeze
       To the insouciant head
              The last *Bless You* drifts to the floor
                     The microbes of apathy spread

MAD COWS AND BENEDICTIONS

Two feet and a mouth steal the last herd
from my father's rented coffin.
The decayed fruit in his throat
swallows the bank notes with a cattleman's pride.

I, a rabbit-faggot, sit in the front row.
My balls of cotton
pewtered between bovines-in-waiting
& clip-on accessories
to past and future crimes.

Chicanery offers me a handkerchief;
I ostensibly blow.

> *Thankless child…*

The minister breathes between *Psalms;*
but I, the hunted heir, hop-a-long toward *Revelations.*

> *Oh, how the hands rustle in Bloomington Township*
> *when the brand irons are asleep!*
> *The 4-hers are a quartet of hoodlums*
> *who dig my daddy's grave deep!*

I stand a pallbearer appalled
& grip the aureate bar.

> *Is this the gold I wanted to touch?*
> *The carat stick which is finally mine?*

Two feet and a mouth steal the last herd
from my father's coffin.

> *Rest uneasily, you best laid plans,*
> *not even the winded rains*
> *obliterate so much terrain,*
> *not even my mother*
> *has such small hands.*

SADNESS IS A PLACE

We learn it as an abstract noun
Intangible to the pupil's optic optimism
Below see-level
An *–ity*, and *–ism*, a *–tude*
A vapor reduced to tears

But Sadness is a place
I have made correspondence of despondence
With its town-and-country face
A miasmic city-state of sorrow
Floating through a deaf sound

Its great, gray smokestacks
Emit monoxide anti-smells
Noxious, noisome
To tickle the passengers in the garage
Too melancholy to complain or cry

Yes, Sadness is a place
You must slow down
To keep up pace
A tourist distraction
Visited by those unafraid of water
With tickets to sigh

THE RESPIRED

Breathing lessons have expired, sound the knell
Death enters the classroom and tweaks your nose
In time you lose the scent but not the smell

The lungs are last to quit and push to swell
The air that you breathe at semester's close
Breathing lessons have expired sound the knell

Oxygen gone, students exit pell-mell
Their huddled bouquet reeks the tone of sorrow
In time you lose the scent but not the smell

So why respire when the throat's afire? Hell,
You'll never learn what the Instructor knows
Breathing lessons have expired, sound the knell

The aroma of darkness absorbs cells
You've earned the course credit now pay off the loan
In time you lose the scent but not the smell

We sniff what the metaphysical sells
Then suffocate beneath trivial stones
Breathing lessons have expired, sound the knell
In time you lose the scent but not the smell

APRIA

Apria should be the name
of a Greek goddess
whose pulchritude lives by a brook,
not the calling card
of an oxygen-delivery company
that leaves a family breathless
when the lungs are unable
to blacken any deeper,
when the deductible has been met;
but assurance pays no more.

Enter, Apria,
for my father has died.
Grace your loveliness
over this house of mourning-pearl interim.
Extend your winged appendages
to collect these tubes, tanks, and belts--
this hospital bed on loan.
Abscond this hardware, my dad's second skin,
from the weathered eyes
of our overcast home.

Then away with you, Apria.
Ascend to your waters
glistening with fresh stone light,
resplendent like a prairie star,
for the strike that has darkened
on this swollen ground,
where because he has been,
we simply are.

FINAL CUT

I was looking for scissors
When I heard the call
Or, more precisely,
Heard the ring
& accepted the call
The voice on the line
One of a male nurse
The news was bad
But it could have been worse

You, the deceased,
A husband to a Nightingale
Who had been flying & dying
To keep you alive
The word of your release
Spread like the field
Of your labors
When you were a young hand
& willing to survive

Placing the receiver
Back on its base,
I wanted to sleep
But walked instead
To the closet of dreams
& selected a suit
Dark blue or black
Perhaps the decision is moot

Father, brother, uncle, grandpa
A quartet of titles
Passed away
In this hour
Of condolences
& euphemisms
Conversations of your pain
& paroxysms

In your era of errors, you were a man of stone;
Then how could you die?
How could your lithic genes
Create a boy with a heart of paper
Such as mine?

To prepare for your leaving,
I brushed up on a vernacular grim,
So I could comprehend
The *You* others knew as *Him*
The codicils, probate process & deeds.
I'll argue for my share.
These unjust desserts & trivial needs

I have found the scissors
Tucked away in my soul
I have the blades of duel
How the pair cuts & we bleed

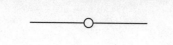